Level 2

The Nature Kid's Guide to SNAKES

DAVID ANDERSON

LP Media Inc. Publishing

For information address LP Media Inc. Publishing,
30012 Variolite St NW, Princeton MN 55371
www.lpmedia.org

Publication Data

Snakes
The Nature Kid's Guide to Snakes — First edition.

Summary: "Learn all about Snakes, the Nature Kid Way"
— Provided by publisher.

ISBN: 979-8-89818-179-6

[1. Snakes - Non-Fiction] I. Title.

Title: The Nature Kid's Guide to Snakes

CONTENTS

SLITHERING SECRETS

DID YOU KNOW?

Snakes live on every continent except Antarctica — it's just too cold there!

Hiss! A long snake slides through the tall green grass.

Snakes live all over the world. They slither through forests, slide across burning deserts, and swim through ponds and rivers. Some are tiny enough to curl up in your hand. Others grow longer than a school bus!

Snakes are **reptiles** with dry, smooth scales that protect their bodies like armor. They use the sun to warm up and rest in cool, hidden spots when it gets too hot or cold.

There are over 3,000 kinds of snakes on Earth. Some are gentle enough to keep as pets. Others are fierce hunters with deadly venom. Get ready to meet some amazing animals!

SCALE AND BONE

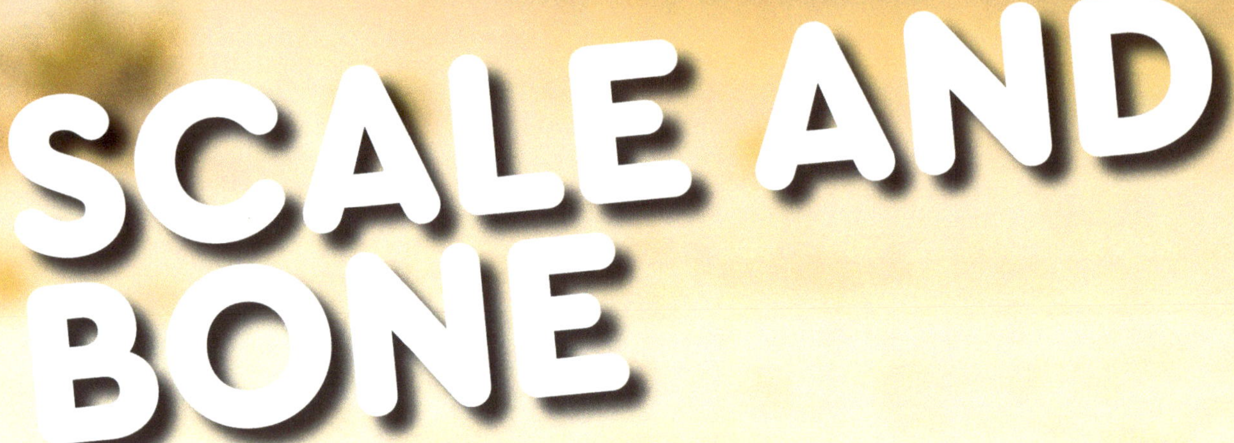

Some snakes have over 200 pairs of ribs — humans only have 12 pairs!

Whoosh! A Saharan horned viper bends and curves across the hot sand.

A snake has a long body but no arms or legs. Its bones are very flexible and bend easily. A large python can have more than 400 of them! That helps it twist, turn, and squeeze into tight spaces.

Different snakes have different types of **scales**. Some feel rough and bumpy, while others are smooth and shiny. As a snake grows, its old skin gets too small, so it sheds it – and a bright, fresh layer waits right underneath!

Snakes move by pushing their belly scales against the ground. Each scale grips like a tiny shoe. That's the secret behind their fast, smooth slither!

DEADLY TACTICS

FUN FACT! After swallowing a big meal, some snakes don't eat again for a whole month!

Squeeze! A boa wraps tight around its prey and holds on.

Snakes catch food in two main ways. Some use **venom**. Others use strong muscles to squeeze.

Venomous snakes have sharp fangs. They bite and push venom into their prey. This makes the prey stop moving fast. Cobras and rattlesnakes hunt this way.

Constrictors take a different approach. They wrap their bodies around prey and squeeze tight. They do not let go until the animal stops breathing. Both boas and pythons are constrictors.

Both ways work well for catching dinner!

HEAT SEEKERS

DID YOU KNOW?

Snakes have no eyelids. They sleep with their eyes wide open!

Flick! A snake's forked tongue tastes the air for clues.

Snakes see the world in a special way. They do not have ears on the outside. But they feel vibrations in the ground through their jaw bones. This tells them when something is near.

A snake flicks its tongue in and out. The forked tip picks up tiny bits from the air. Then it brings them to a special spot in the mouth. This helps the snake smell and taste at once!

Some snakes can even sense heat from other animals. Rattlesnakes have small pits on their face for this. They can hunt in total darkness. It's like they have built-in night-vision goggles!

GARTER GATHERINGS

FUN FACT! A scared garter snake releases a stinky smell from its tail. It smells like rotten eggs!

Zip! A garter snake zips through the garden after a frog.

Garter snakes are one of the most common snakes in North America. You might spot one in a yard, park, or near a pond. They have colorful stripes that run down their body from head to tail.

These snakes eat frogs, worms, and slugs. They are small and gentle. Many people keep them as pets because they are easy to care for.

When cold months arrive, garter snakes gather in big groups. Hundreds may curl up together in one underground den! They share body heat to stay warm all winter long.

CORNFIELD COLORS

DID YOU KNOW?

Corn snakes are amazing climbers — they can crawl straight up a brick wall!

Rustle! A bright orange corn snake peeks out from the hay.

Corn snakes are named for the farms where they were often found. They hunt mice and rats in barns and fields. Their orange and red marks look a bit like kernels of corn.

Corn snakes are calm and gentle. They make great first pets for snake lovers! They just need a glass tank with a warm lamp and a cozy place to hide.

Pet corn snakes eat small mice about once a week. They need fresh water every day. With good care, a corn snake can live for over 20 years. That is a long friendship!

WATER MOCCASINS

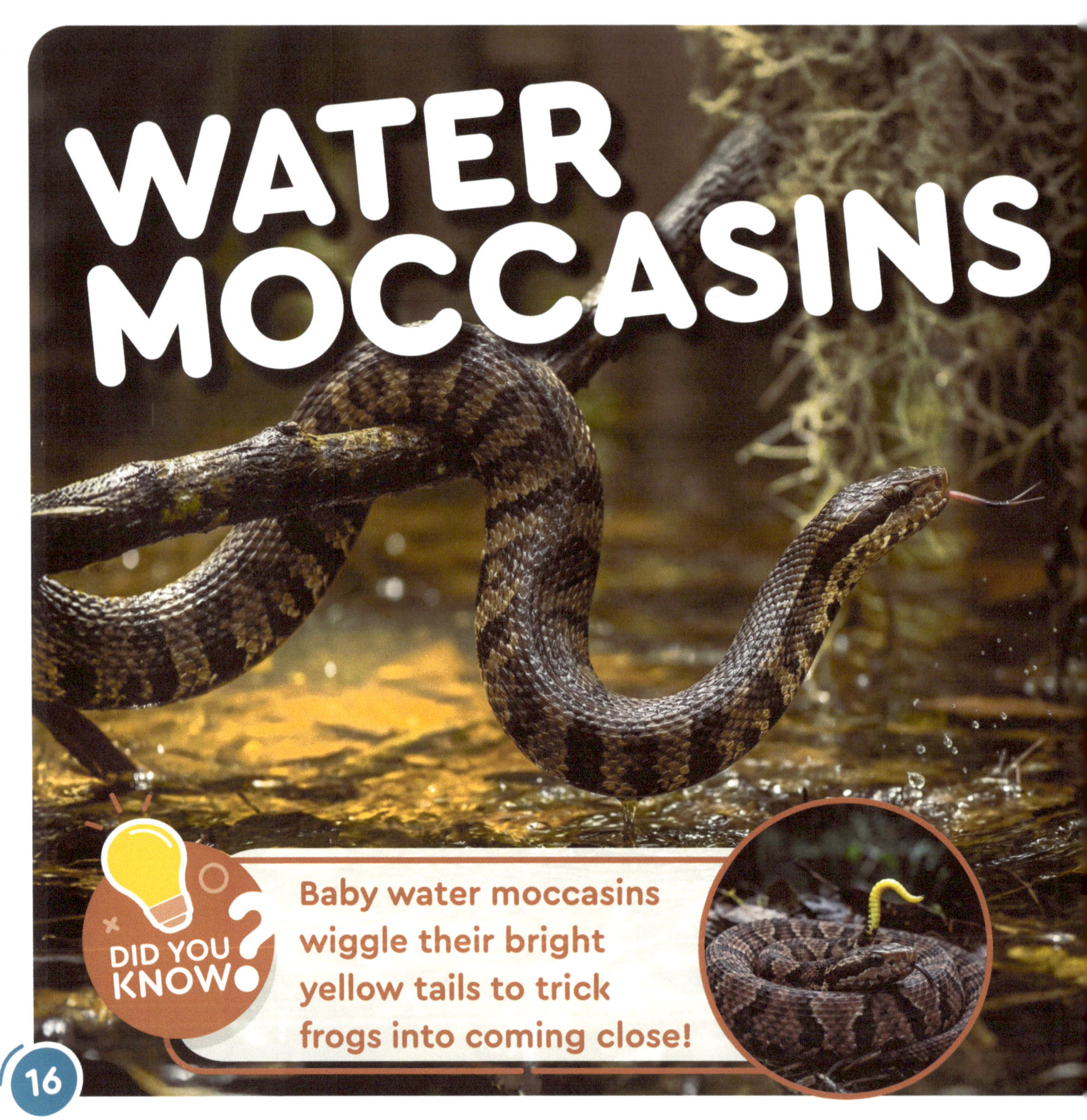

DID YOU KNOW?

Baby water moccasins wiggle their bright yellow tails to trick frogs into coming close!

Splash! A water moccasin drops from a branch into the swamp.

Water moccasins live near swamps, lakes, and streams in the southeastern United States. They are also called cottonmouths. When scared, they open their mouth wide. The inside is bright white like cotton!

These snakes are strong swimmers. They glide across the water with their head held high, looking for food. They eat fish, frogs, and small animals.

Water moccasins are venomous, so it is best to stay far away. If you see one, do not try to touch it. Just walk away slowly and let it be.

RATTLE READY

FUN FACT!

A rattlesnake can shake its rattle up to 60 times per second — so fast it just looks like a blur!

Rattle, rattle! A rattlesnake shakes its tail as a warning.

Rattlesnakes are famous for the rattle at the end of their tail. When they shake it, it makes a loud buzzing sound — like a warning alarm. Other animals know to back off when they hear it!

The rattle is made of loose rings of hard skin called keratin. That's the same material as your fingernails! Each time a rattlesnake sheds its skin, a new ring is added to the rattle. The more rings, the louder the buzz.

Rattlesnakes are venomous. They strike fast when they feel in danger. But most of the time, they just want to be left alone. That rattle is their way of saying "please go away!"

HOGNOSE HIJINKS

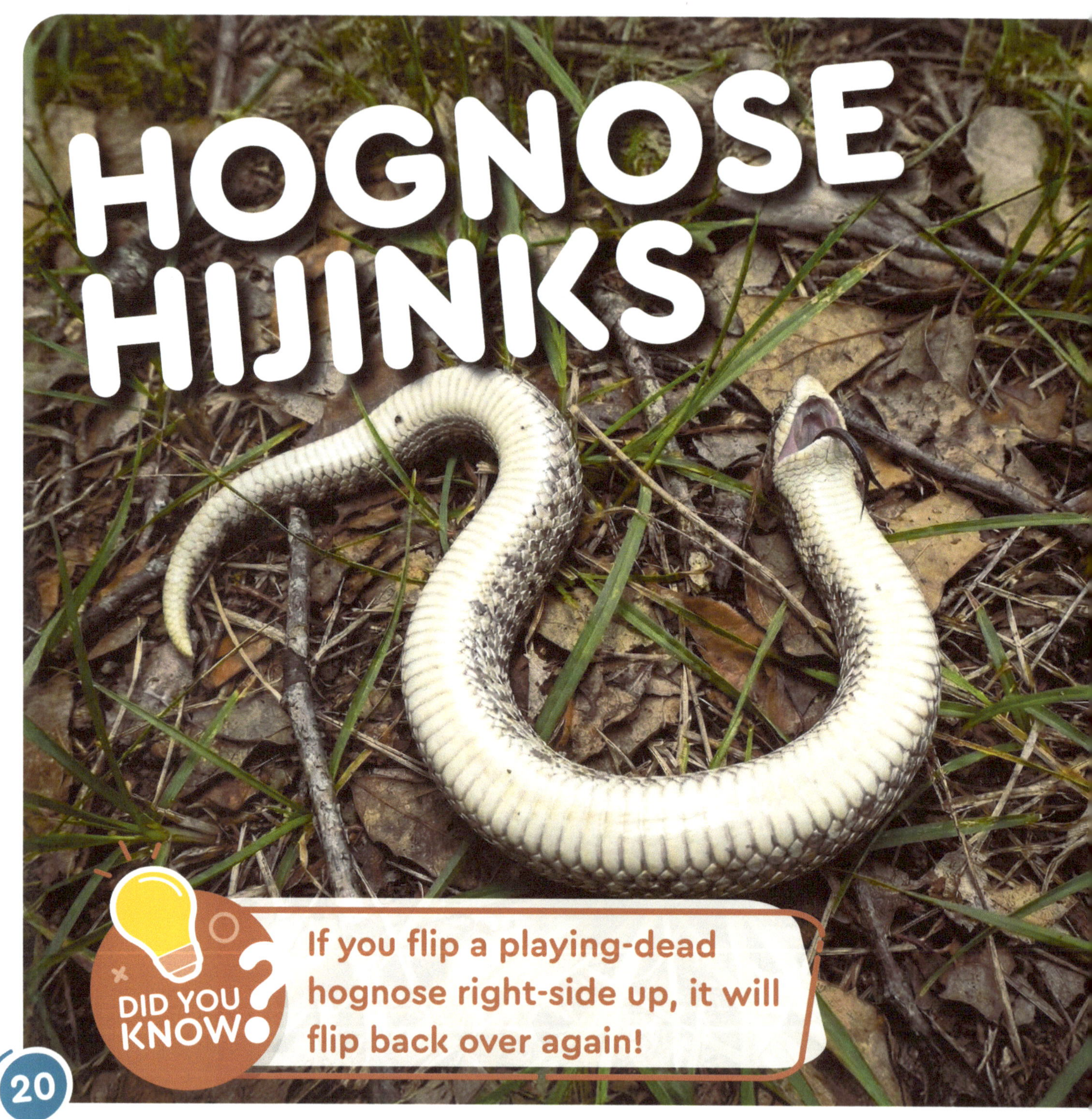

DID YOU KNOW?

If you flip a playing-dead hognose right-side up, it will flip back over again!

Flop! A hognose snake rolls on its back and plays dead.

Hognose snakes have a cute turned-up nose. It looks a bit like a pig snout! They use it to dig in loose dirt and find toads to eat.

When a hognose snake is scared, it puts on a big show. First, it puffs up and hisses loudly. If that does not work, it flips onto its back, opens its mouth, and plays dead! It even lets its tongue hang out.

Hognose snakes are gentle and totally harmless. Some people even keep them as pets! With that silly nose and all those dramatic moves, it is easy to see why so many kids love them.

SIDEWAYS SLITHER

FUN FACT!

When a sidewinder moves, only two small spots on its body touch the hot sand at a time!

Swish! A sidewinder scoots across the hot desert sand.

Sidewinders live in hot, sandy deserts. They are a type of rattlesnake. But they move in a very strange way. Instead of going straight, they toss their body sideways!

This odd movement helps them travel over loose sand without sinking in. They leave wavy J-shaped lines behind them. It almost looks like tire tracks in the desert!

Sidewinders hunt at night when the desert cools down. They eat lizards, mice, and small birds. Their sandy color helps them blend in perfectly with the ground.

COBRA KINGS

DID YOU KNOW?

A king cobra's venom is strong enough to bring down an elephant with one bite!

Hiss! A king cobra rises up and spreads its wide hood.

King cobras are the longest venomous snakes in the world. They can grow up to 18 feet long. That is about as long as a car!

A scared king cobra lifts its body off the ground. It can raise up high enough to look a grown person in the eye! Then it spreads the skin near its head into a wide hood. This makes it look big and scary.

King cobras live in forests in Asia. They mostly eat other snakes, even venomous ones. They are the only snakes that build nests for their eggs and guard them until they hatch.

MAMBA MENACE

DID YOU KNOW?

A black mamba can lift its head four feet off the ground. That's as high as a kitchen counter!

Surprise! A black mamba opens its mouth wide — the inside is pitch black!

Black mambas are one of the fastest snakes on Earth. They can move at up to 12 miles per hour. That is faster than most people can run!

But black mambas are not actually black! Their skin is gray or brown. But the inside of their mouth is inky black. That is how they got their name.

Black mambas live in Africa. They are shy and try to avoid people. But their venom is very strong, so people stay far away when they see a speedy black mamba slithering by!

ANACONDA AMBUSH

FUN FACT!

A green anaconda can hold its breath underwater for up to ten minutes while waiting for prey!

Shhh! A green anaconda slithers quietly across a river.

Green anacondas are the heaviest snakes in the world. They can weigh over 500 pounds. That is as heavy as a big lion!

These huge snakes live in rivers and swamps in South America. They are great swimmers. Their eyes and nose sit on top of their head, like a crocodile. This lets them hide in the water and watch for **prey**.

Anacondas squeeze their prey with great force. They can eat animals as big as deer or wild pigs! After a huge meal, they may rest for weeks while they digest.

PYTHON PATTERNS

FUN FACT!

Reticulated pythons are such strong swimmers that they cross miles of open ocean to reach tiny islands far out at sea!

Creak! A huge python loops around a thick tree branch.

Reticulated pythons are the longest snakes in the world. They can grow over 20 feet long — and some have been found stretching over 30 feet. That is longer than a school bus!

This snake's skin has a beautiful pattern of gold, brown, and black shapes. The word reticulated means net-like. The pattern helps them hide among leaves and branches in the forest.

Reticulated pythons live in Southeast Asia. They are great swimmers and climbers. They catch prey by waiting very still, then striking fast. Patience is their secret weapon.

SOARING SERPENTS

DID YOU KNOW?

Flying snakes actually glide better than flying squirrels — they're nature's best gliders!

Whip! A flying snake launches itself from a high branch. It's gliding!

Flying snakes do not really fly. But they can glide through the air! They live in the trees of Southeast Asia and rarely come down to the ground.

To take off, a flying snake crawls to the end of a branch. Then it jumps! It flattens its body like a ribbon and sucks in its belly. This creates a shape that catches the air.

Flying snakes can glide over 100 feet in a single leap. They steer by wiggling their body in the air. Scientists are still studying how these amazing snakes do it!

DEEP SEA SWIMMERS

Sea snakes can dive over 300 feet deep — that's deeper than the Statue of Liberty is tall!

Swoosh! A sea snake slips through the warm ocean waves.

Sea snakes spend most of their lives in the ocean. They have a flat tail shaped like a paddle. This tail works like a fin, pushing them through the water with ease.

Most sea snakes are venomous. But they are gentle and rarely bite people. They eat fish and eels that live near coral reefs.

Sea snakes can't breathe underwater. They still need to come up to the surface to breathe air. But some can hold their breath for over two hours! They live in warm oceans near Asia and Australia, where the water stays nice and toasty.

FRIENDLY SNAKES

DID YOU KNOW?

Doctors use snake venom to make medicine that helps save people from heart attacks!

Shhh! A girl gently holds her pet ball python in her hands.

People and snakes have lived side by side for thousands of years. In many cultures, snakes stand for wisdom and healing. You can even see them on some doctor signs!

Snakes help people in big ways. They eat rats and mice that damage crops and spread disease. Without snakes, there would be many more pests in our world.

Some snakes make great pets. Corn snakes and ball pythons are gentle and easy to handle. With good care, a snake can be a great pet for many years.

SERPENT SALUTE

FUN FACT!

The Barbados thread snake is so tiny it can curl up on top of a quarter!

Crack! A tiny snake breaks through its shell and sees the world.

Snakes are some of the coolest animals on Earth. They have been around for over 100 million years! From tiny thread snakes to giant pythons, they come in all shapes, sizes, and colors.

Many people fear snakes. But most snakes are shy and just want to be left alone. Learning about them can help turn fear into wonder.

You can help snakes by respecting wild places and never bothering a snake you find outside. Every snake plays an important role in keeping our world healthy and balanced, and now you know just how amazing they really are.

GLOSSARY

reptile
An animal with scales that uses the sun to stay warm.

scales
Small, flat plates that cover a snake's body.

venom
Poison that some snakes use to stop their prey.

prey
An animal that is hunted and eaten by another animal.

constrictor
A snake that squeezes its prey to catch it.

www.ingramcontent.com/pod-product-compliance
Lightning Source LLC
LaVergne TN
LVHW071209160826
845679LV00003B/780

* 9 7 9 8 8 9 8 1 8 1 7 9 6 *